# Introduction

When you have read this, I hope you will feel that, if an eighty year old can entertain without fuss and produce delicious food, you can too. And there is no need to wait until you are eighty; it is just as good at much younger ages. Elaborate entertaining is not essential; the important thing is to spend time with your guests and enjoy their company. I know some people who try elaborate recipes. When they succeed it is a triumph, but when it goes wrong it is a disaster. None of the recipes that follow can go seriously wrong. the worst that can happen is that when serving a stew, the sauce is too runny. For this there is a foolproof emergency procedure. Take two heaped teaspoons of arrowroot, mix them with milk and add to the stew, stirring; within a minute the sauce will have thickened beautifully. Nobody need know that you have used arrowroot.

After my wife died I made the firm decision that I was going to entertain regularly and make new friends. Underlying this decision was also a feeling that if I was going to live here alone, I had an obligation to share the beauty of the house and the garden with others. Having people to lunch and dinner was a start, but I needed to do more. I joined a scheme known as "Invitation to View" in 2004 when Buxlow was one of 32 country houses in Suffolk who opened their houses and gardens on certain specified days in the year. I opened on one day in April and two in June inviting guests to come at 5 pm; they had a talk from me about the house, the garden and the family, followed by a guided tour of garden and house (there were twenty guests on all three occasions) and they were then offered canapés and wine (still white wine or cava or Duchy Original apple refresher). The excellent canapés were provided by a local caterer - Country Cuisine. But because it is something of a trade mark for me, I also provided some of my own home made bruschetta with pesto. The recipe will follow!

In 2006 Buxlow is now one of 39 houses in Suffolk - and now, for the first time, also in Essex, Cambridgeshire and Norfolk - and I shall be opening on four days, adding another one towards the end of September.

For six years now I have been entertaining a growing number of friends to lunches and dinners. In my eightieth year I realised that I could not remember what I had given guests to eat the previous time they had been and began to record all my entertaining with the names of guests and the meals we had eaten. On several occasions guest have asked

me for recipes of one dish or another. But it was only on the most recent occasion that one of the guests said "Guy, you really ought to write a book of your recipes". And it was that remark that has prompted this short book.

Before I describe the meals and give recipes, I should say something about my cooking. I have always liked good food. I even remember some of the lunches served at the school in Belgium where I was from the age of 5 to 8; pork with prunes particularly appealed to me. I was not brought up by my parents; my father was in the Malayan Civil Service and I was sent back to Europe at the age of 5. Aunty Claire, who was my guardian, was a competent cook, but not inspiring. However, another aunt, Kathleen, with whose family I spent many holidays in the 1930s, was a wonderful cook and managed splendid meals in a house with no running water, no electricity and a paraffin stove with two hobs and an oven. I watched what went on and absorbed the basics without actually being taught. My grandmother, a French Mauritian also loved food. One of her specialities, which I loved was a cauliflower salad. I learned this about 70 years ago:

# Granny's Cauliflower Salad

Cut a cauliflower into wedges and steam until tender, but still firm.

## For the dressing

Hard boil two eggs. Separate the whites and the yolk. Mash the yolks with olive oil; add more oil, squeeze in the juice of half a lemon, add a dash of double cream, add the finely chopped whites of egg, season with salt and pepper and stir well. It should be full-bodied but quite runny.

Serve the cauliflower portions and hand the dressing in a sauceboat.

This is the way I always used to cook it, but I now prefer to cook cauliflower in a different way. Break the cauliflower into florets; cut large florets in half so that all the florets are about the same size. Put them in boiling water, bring back to the boil and cook for 6 minutes. Drain in a sieve and hold under running cold water for about a minute and allow to drain. Cool in the fridge. Cauliflower cooked this way can also be reheated in a cheese sauce and served with meat.

I am often asked when I first started cooking. I couldn't remember, but my sister tells me that when we were camping on a fruit farm in Sussex during the Battle of Britain in September 1940 I shared all the cooking with another girl. I can't think what we cooked. Food rationing was severe. It must have included potatoes baked in the warm ash of the camp fire and possibly under the counter sausages. Four years later at the age of nineteen, as one of four Sergeants in a small unit fighting the Japanese in the jungle of the Kabaw Valley in Burma, I found myself the cook again. This time all our food was dropped to us from the air in large 'compo' tins. All I had to do was light a camp fire and heat the tins of M&V (meat & vegetables); this I did in an ancient kettle - Heaven knows where that came from!

When we first lived in America, in 1953-4 we discovered Mrs. Rombauer's "The Joy of Cooking", from which I still use recipes; later on I shall give her recipe for Pumpkin Pie, adapted for use with a food processor. When we lived in Virginia, just across the Potomac from Washington DC, in the late 1950s, I remember I used to long for our Jamaican maid's day off, so that I could get in to the kitchen!

Finally a word about what one might call my 'rules of engagement' in entertaining. I became fairly deaf in about 1996 and use hearing aids, but I cannot follow the conversation if there are too many people talking at the same time. So I try and limit my lunches and dinners to five people, with me at the end of the able and two guests on either side of me, But I do go up to six, and at Christmas, with a lot of the family present, we have even more. That sometimes means that I sit at my end of the table enjoying the sight of my guests eating and talking, but not actually being able to make out a word of what they are saying. So you will find that most of my recipes are for 4-6 people. Some of the dishes are quite ample and there is often enough left over for me to have for supper the next day.

I usually serve four courses, including cheese as a course. But I aim to spend as much time as possible with my guests. I don't want to have to disappear to the kitchen for long periods. So I aim to produce meals, usually with a cold starter and a main course which can be prepared in advance - quite often the day before. Main courses can be reheated before the guests arrive and then kept warm on hot plates; many main courses are in fact better the next day. I don't like to sit down to lunch much later than 1 o'clock and to dinner much later than 8.15, so I always invite my guest for 12.30 for lunch and 7.30 for dinner. When it is light, at lunchtime and at dinner in the summer, we usually have a short walk round the garden before coming in to talk over cava (the Catalonian sparkling wine) with mûre (blackberry liqueur) and bruschetta with my home made pesto. Most people put too much mûre in with the cava; it should be just enough to give the cava a pink tinge - rather like the angostura bitters in a pink gin. Following is the recipe for bruschetta with pesto.

# Bruschetta with Pesto

Heat the oven - 190 Celsius, fan assisted. Brush slices of bread with olive oil on both sides and place them on a rack over a baking tray; put them in the oven until golden and crisp - about 12 minutes. This can be done some time ahead. Spread the slices of baked bread with a generous spread of pesto. Cut the baked bread into smaller portions for serving. I have tried baking the bread the day before. It remains crisp but is impossible to cut neatly into smaller pieces. So prepare it earlier in the day and spread the pesto an hour or two before needed. I have found from experience that the bruschetta are still crisp 1 ½ hours after spreading the pesto.

## To make the Pesto

The basic recipe was learnt by my daughter Amicia at a course at the Aldeburgh Cookery School. But I have adapted - and improved it. This makes more than one would need for 6 or fewer guests, but provided it is covered with cling film it will last for at least a week in the fridge and can be used for pasta with pesto.
Or it can be frozen.

- Fill the bowl of a medium sized food processor with basil leaves, and I do mean fill. You have to pack it in, stalks and all.
- Add 2 oz of grated parmesan cheese, or if you can get hold of it, combine equal quantities of parmesan and peccorino cheese.
- A small handful of pine nuts
- A small handful of walnuts
- 2 cloves of garlic, skinned and chopped.
- Salt and pepper.

Whizz until finely ground and then, whilst still whizzing, slowly add ¼ pint of extra virgin olive oil. And, that's it.

As a variant, I sometimes make the pesto with rocket instead of basil.

I buy a lot of organic vegetables; not because I think they taste any different, but because I like to use really fresh food and two organic farms, Maple Farm and Peakhill Farm, are just down the road from me and I know that everything I get from them has just been picked. I buy all my meat locally, most of it grown in Suffolk. Fish is a bit of a problem since the fishermen in Aldeburgh are being driven out of business by EU regulations. I usually buy from Darren and Wendy who have a stall in Saxmundham on two days a week; they come from Lowestoft.

I don't do a great range of puddings. I have always been keener on savoury dishes. I have to admit that I do on occasions serve bought puddings - mainly the Cartmel Village Stores sticky toffee and sticky ginger puddings.

The following recipes include all that have been served by me in the last 2 ½ years together with some favourite recipes which for some reason or other have not been served recently.

# Starters
## Smoked eel on toast

It is easy - in Suffolk - to buy fillets of smoked eel. But they are too thin for my taste. I like fillets at least a ¼ inch thick. So I buy whole smoked eels. The skin is easily removed - like peeling off a glove. Cut sufficient fillets to cover two pieces of toast per person. I use a bread called 'grand rustique' (quite why it's called 'grand' I don't know since each slice is only about 6" x 2½").

Spread each piece of toast with a generous helping of horseradish sauce. Lay on the eel fillets. Two pieces of toast to each plate and scatter over wild rocket. I once served this to a lady who asked me after she had eaten it what it was. When I said 'eel', she said "If you had told me in advance, I couldn't have brought myself to eat it. Eel sounds disgusting, but, thank you, it was delicious."

# Gravadlax

I always make my own gravadlax

- 2 tail end pieces of filleted salmon with the skin still on.
- 4 tbsps fine sea salt
- 2 tbsps caster sugar
- 2 tbsps coarsely ground white pepper
- a large bunch of fresh dill, finely chopped

Mix the salt, sugar and pepper. (Don't use commercially ground white pepper) Sprinkle some chopped dill in the bottom of a dish which will hold the salmon without folding it. ( I use a pyrex dish which will take two pieces 10 inches long).

Place one piece of salmon skin side down in the dish; sprinkle it lavishly with dill and the salting mixture. Place the second piece of salmon on it skin side up. Sprinkle the top with the remaining dill and salt mixture.

Cover the fish with folded aluminium foil and refrigerate under a weight of approximately 2 lbs. I use the weights from an old fashioned weighing scale.

Refrigerate for not less than 36 hours and up to three or four days, turning the fish every 12 hours and basting it with the juices that will run from the fish.

Remove the weights and the foil, scrape off the curing mixture. Dry the fish and slice it on the diagonal like smoked salmon. But don't slice it paper thin; I much prefer chunky slices (like the smoked eel). I find that one of the pieces is ample for 4 to 6 people and I freeze the other piece (unsliced) for another occasion. Serve with buttered brown bread and hand gravlax sauce.

# Gravlaxsäs

- 2 tbsps dijon mustard
- 1 tbsp caster sugar
- 2 dstsps white wine vinegar
- salt and freshly ground white pepper
- 2 to 3 fl oz of mild vegetable oil
- 3 tbsps chopped fresh dill

Mix the mustard, sugar, salt, pepper and vinegar in a bowl and beat in the oil slowly to make a smooth, creamy dressing; stir in the dill and serve in a sauce boat or spoon onto each plate.

Keeping, as I now do, a book of the menus I have served to guests, I was able to discover that I had given four guests gravadlax as a starter on a previous occasion, so to make a change this time, I gave them scrambled eggs with it - having successfully tried that out the evening before! Just one egg per person, cooked a moment before serving. It goes very well.

Just a word here on scrambled eggs. I like to see a clear mixture of cooked white and cooked yolk. So I do not beat the eggs, but break the eggs into hot butter - in a non-stick pan - and let it start cooking for a moment or two before beginning to scramble with a wooden spoon over a very low heat. It looks so much more attractive than the usual method.

# Roast Aldeburgh asparagus

Allow six stems of asparagus per person. Hold each asparagus stem in both hands with the tip to your left (if right-handed), snap off the hard end; it will always break at just the right point. What is left is entirely edible - no need to hold the asparagus in one hand when eating. The asparagus can be eaten with a knife and fork. And no need for finger bowls.

- Preheat the oven to 200 degrees celsius.
- Lay the stems on a flat baking tray and sprinkle with olive oil; use your fingers to coat each stem; Put the tray in the oven for 15 minutes.
- Remove and sprinkle the asparagus with balsamic vinegar and freshly grated parmesan cheese.
- Serve six pieces to each guest.

As a variant try roast asparagus with vanilla flavoured olive oil. Vanilla flavoured olive oil is available commercially, but I now make my own, putting two long pods of vanilla in a small bottle and topping it up with extra virgin olive oil. Use after a month.

NB At the end of the asparagus season, I always buy several pounds of asparagus; break off the hard end of each stem and freeze. Lay the pieces flat on a baking tray to freeze. When frozen put them into a freezer bag (12 pieces in each bag). They can be used for roasting and can be roasted from frozen; just allow twenty minutes in a hot oven. Frozen asparagus cannot satisfactorily be steamed; it becomes mushy.

# Asparagus with sauce mousseline

Prepare the asparagus in the same way as for roast asparagus. Place in a steamer and steam for about ten minutes. Place them on plates and hand sauce mousseline (hollandaise sauce with whipped cream folded in).

Hollandaise is a bit tedious to make the correct way. Here is a much easier recipe taken from a book that my son had at University, called "Super Scoff".

Put 3 egg yolks into a liquidiser, add a few drops of of lemon juice and 1 tablespoon of water. Blend for a minute and then pour in very slowly 6 oz of boiling butter. Remove from the liquidiser and whisk with a wire whisk, adding seasoning as required.

# Artichokes

Young globe artichokes can, in this country, only be obtained if home grown. They are picked when they are smaller than my fist (which is quite large!). At this age there is no 'choke' to be removed. Most people serve globe artichokes with melted butter. I find it messy and frankly not very tasty. I serve them with sauce mousseline. Small young artichokes don't need to be boiled for more than about 15 minutes.

# Chilled cucumber and lovage soup

- 1 large onion, peeled and chopped
- 1 cucumber, peeled and diced
- a good handful of lovage leaves
- 1 scant litre of chicken stock and cream to taste

In a large saucepan, melt a large chunk of unsalted butter, soften the onion. Add the cucumber and stew for at least ten minutes. Add the stock and bring to the boil, simmer for 5 minutes. Add the roughly chopped lovage leaves and simmer for a minute more. Season to taste.

Cool the liquid. Process it in a blender. Return to the pan. If the liquid is too runny, reduce it, before adding single cream to taste.

Remove from the pan, pouring it into a bowl. Refrigerate for at least one hour and serve.

It is worth mentioning at this point that there is a dish known as Trout Doria which is trout served with stewed cucumber. It was a favourite of my wife's, and I always livened it up by adding chopped lovage to the cucumber.

# Courgette soup  (adapted from Katie Stewart)

- 1 oz of unsalted butter
- 1 large onion, finely chopped
- 1 lb of courgettes
- 1 ½ pints of chicken stock

Melt the butter in a large saucepan. Add the finely chopped onion and sauté gently for about five minutes until the onion is soft but not brown.

Trim and slice the courgettes, add to the pan and mix with the onion and butter and sauté for another five minutes. Stir in the chicken stock and bring to the boil. Cover and simmer gently for 30 minutes. Draw off the heat and let it cool. Purée in a blender. Return to the pan, check the seasoning, add a few tablespoonfuls of single cream, reheat and serve. It is also very good as a chilled soup.

# Palestine Soup

*(This recipe comes from Jane Grigson's Vegetable Book)*

- 1 lb large Jerusalem artichokes
- 1 large onion, chopped
- 1 clove of garlic, chopped
- ½ stick of celery, chopped
- 4 oz of butter
- 2 rashers of Suffolk sweet cured back bacon, or 2 oz of ham
- 1 litre of light chicken stock
- 8 fl oz of milk
- 6 tbsps of cream
- chopped parsley and chives

Jerusalem artichokes are not easy to prepare. Jane Grigson recommends boiling them and then rubbing off the peel. I prefer to peel them raw with a potato peeler. The newer varieties of Jerusalem artichokes tend to be rounder and less knobbly than they used to be and this makes peeling easier.

Cut up the artichokes. Put them in a large pan with the onion, garlic and celery with half the butter. Cover tightly and stew over a low heat for ten minutes, giving the pan an occasional shake. Now add the chopped bacon or ham and cook a moment or two longer. Pour in the stock and simmer until all the vegetables are soft. Process in the blender. Reheat, adding milk to dilute to taste, but don't dilute too much; the consistency should be creamy. Correct the seasoning. Stir in the last of the butter, the cream and herbs.

Serve with croutons of fried bread in butter

Jerusalem artichokes have nothing to do with Jerusalem or with Palestine. 'Jerusalem' is just a typical English garbling of the Italian 'girasole' - sunflower (literally - turns with the sun).

# Terrine de foie banque

*(So named because the recipe was given to me by a chef who was the son of one of my colleagues in the Bank of England, thirty years ago)*

- 1 lb chicken livers
- 8 oz pig's liver
- 8 oz veal
- 1 lb sausage meat
- 2 medium onions
- 2 cloves of garlic
- 5 tbsps of oil
- 2 egg yolks
- 12 oz streaky bacon
- a small handful of black peppercorns
- salt and pepper
- herbs (suggested sage, thyme, basil, marjoram, dill)
- 1 bottle miniature brandy

Set aside a large bowl. Mince the chicken liver in the food processor and tip into the bowl. Mince the veal and tip into the bowl. Chop the pig's liver and tip into the bowl. Add the sausage meat and mix all the meats together with a wooden spoon.

Finely chop the onions and garlic and fry them in oil in a large deep stew pan until just beginning to colour. Now add the meat from the bowl, two large spoonfuls at a time, and keep stir frying. Make sure that it is all done, but not overdone.

In the meantime, flatten the bacon rashers with the blade of a large kitchen knife. Line a suitable terrine or loaf tin with the bacon, placing the peppercorns underneath.

Mix the egg yolks, brandy and herbs, seasoned with salt and black pepper, and add to the meat and onion mixture and place in the terrine, already lined.

Place in a bain-marie (if you don't have a bain-marie, use a deep roasting pan with water to about half way up the terrine). Put in an oven set at 170 Celsius (fan assisted) and bake for ¾ of an hour. Turn the oven off and leave the terrine in the oven to cool off - about 2 hours. Place a sheet of foil over the terrine and weight it.

Keep in the fridge for 48 hours. To serve, run the blade of a flexible knife round the edge of the terrine several times, exerting a lifting motion, Now turn the terrine upside down and turn the contents on to a platter. Cut into slices and serve with toast.

You will have more than enough for six guests. Place the rest on a large piece of foil, wrap carefully and freeze for another day.

# Risottos

These can be either a starter or a main course. Adjust the quantities as appropriate.

# Wild mushrooms

Depending on the season of the year I use either dried fungi porcini and dried morels, or I use various wild mushrooms picked around here. Sometimes they are served fresh; or I use a variety of mushrooms that I have stored in the freezer, including:

**Blewits**, either field or meadow. Delicious and again unmistakable - they are the only blue mushrooms. Known in France as 'pieds bleus'. They appear in late October/ November and can survive frosts. In 2006 I actually picked 10 ounces of blewits on January 22nd!

**St. George's mushrooms** (so called because they appeared on St. George's Day, but with the change to the Julian calendar in the 18th Century, they now tend to appear 11 days later, that is in early May). Unmistakable, since they are the only large mushrooms (white) which appear in late April/early May.

**The Miller**, a large mushroom with a grey top, hence its name - 'dusty miller'. Occurs in October.

**Boletus**, there are various edible varieties. Boletus edulis is the French cep or the Italian porcini. Boletus baddius is almost as good; another closely related mushroom is 'Slippery Jack'.

**Horse mushrooms and field mushrooms.** These are both delicious; the horse mushroom (much larger) has a better flavour.

# Wild mushroom risotto

- 1 large onion, finely chopped
- 12 oz of arborio rice
- 12 oz of wild mushrooms, sliced, may be mixed with dried or frozen mushrooms. When using dried mushrooms, soak them in warm water for half an hour
- 1 ½ litres of chicken stock - the Knorr liquid stock will do
- a splash of white wine
- unsalted butter
- 2 cloves of garlic, crushed
- a handful of grated parmesan cheese

In a thick bottomed deep pan (I use an SKK Alu-guss titanium pan from Cucina Direct) melt a good knob of butter and soften the chopped onion.

Add the sliced fresh mushrooms (and the sliced frozen mushrooms, if using them) and soften. At this stage add any dried mushrooms, reserving the water from the dried and frozen mushrooms.

Now add the rice and stir, coating every grain with the butter. Splash in the white wine and stir till it is absorbed by the rice.

For about 25 minutes cook stirring all the time adding, first, the water from the dried or frozen mushrooms and then the hot stock (from a simmering pan) ladle by ladle. If, like me, you are not going to eat immediately, keep it fairly liquid at the end.

Add some chunks of unsalted butter and a large handful of parmesan cheese and stir till melted. Cover and keep warm on a hot plate.

Keep some warm stock in a pan. Just before serving, pour in a little stock and ensure that the consistency is moist enough. Serve with a green salad.

## Horse mushrooms and/or field mushrooms with toast

- As many mushrooms as you can pick
- 1 pkt of cubetti di pancetta
- 1 small onion
- 2 cloves of garlic crushed and chopped
- olive oil and butter
- a splash of white wine

In a large frying pan heat the pancetta until the fat begins to run. Add the chopped onion and the garlic and stir. Add some butter and olive oil and stir until the onion is soft. Now add the mushrooms cut into pieces and stir over a high heat until the mushrooms have softened. Now a splash of white wine and let it evaporate almost completely. Serve with toast. If there are more mushrooms than you need, the cooked mushrooms can be kept in the fridge for a day or two and reheated. Blewits are very good cooked this way too.

## Parasol mushrooms

Discard the stalk and cut the mushroom into wedges. Dip the wedges into a lightly beaten egg; coat them with bread crumbs and fry over a high heat in butter or oil until crisp and brown on both sides. Serve with mayonnaise.

## Pumpkin Risotto with truffle oil

Pumpkin risotto is a very good dish on its own, but the addition of truffle oil transforms it into a very special dish. I have for some time used a recipe for pumpkin risotto, but the truffle oil was a new idea. It came from Carla Carlisle's Spectator column in Country Life. She was saying how comforting it was when feeling low to cook yourself pumpkin risotto with truffle oil. She did not give a recipe, but here is mine:

(for five persons)
- About 8 oz of cubed peeled pumpkin
- 8 oz of arborio risotto rice
- 1 chopped onion
- 1 small packet of cubeti di pancetta or two rashers of good streaky bacon chopped
- 1 litre of chicken stock
- a generous teaspoon of truffle oil
- parmesan cheese to taste
- 2 oz of butter

Heat the pancetta until the fat begins to run. Add the chopped onion and stir until softened. Add about an ounce of butter and the cubed pumpkin (for how to cook a pumpkin see the recipe for Pumpkin Pie) and stir until the pumpkin is soft (about 10 minutes). Add the arborio rice and stir until the rice is coated with butter. Add a ladleful of hot stock and stir until it has been absorbed. Repeat with the rest of the stock until absorbed, but not too dry; keep the stock simmering in a saucepan. At this point stir in the truffle oil. Season to taste and add the grated parmesan and the rest of the butter. Cover and let it rest for about five minutes. Sprinkle it with chopped parsley and serve.

Blewits

St. George's Mushroom

# Horse Mushrooms

Horse Mushroom 12"x9"

# Main Courses
## Goulash

- 1 ½ - 2 l bs of beef - on this occasion local red poll beef
- 3 oz of lard (or goose fat)
- 1 lb of onions
- 2 tbsps paprika
- 2 tbsps flour
- 1 pint tomato juice
- herbs - bay leaf, rosemary and thyme
- 2 cloves of garlic
- salt
- 1 tsp of caraway seeds
- 1 lb of small scrubbed new potatoes
- 2 squirts of tomato purée
- 2 tbsps of yoghourt

These are the ingredients as given in a very old newspaper cutting - probably the Evening Standard of forty years ago. To it we have added:
- 1 cup of frozen garden peas

Cut the beef into cubes; beef is much tastier if cut into fairly large cubes, at least one inch square. Brown the beef over a hot flame in the lard (or goose fat). Remove the beef, set aside. Put the sliced onions and crushed garlic in the pan and and cook until golden brown. Put back the beef and blend in the flour and the paprika. Add enough liquid (water or tomato juice) to cover, salt to taste and add the caraway seeds and the herbs.

Cover and cook slowly over a moderate heat for at least an hour. The old recipe calls for cooking in the oven (and those with Agas may well wish to do so), but I prefer my titanium deep stewing pan. If cooking on the hob, return from time to time and stir to ensure that it is not sticking.

Now add the small new potatoes and cook for another half an hour. Ensure that the stew is not too dry. Add the cupful of green peas and cook for three more minutes. Finally blend in the tomato puree and the yoghourt.

Keep warm on a hot plate until the guests are ready. I don't think this needs any accompaniment. My guests always serve themselves from the hot plate on the sideboard and I find that if I offer a side salad, guests frequently pile it on to the same plate as the goulash. No Hungarian would ever eat goulash in such a way. If you want a salad, have it separately, afterwards.

# Sweetbreads and morels in a white wine sauce
**Served with Basmati rice and spinach**

Two important points about sweetbreads. First ensure in advance that your guests are happy to eat sweetbreads; many people have doubts about all forms of offal, but sweetbreads, for some reason, seem to be particularly unpopular. My daughter won't touch them; but my guests on this particular evening were all accustomed to sweetbreads.

Secondly, many butchers in England are still under the impression that they are not allowed to sell veal sweetbreads and can only sell lamb's sweetbreads. But veal sweetbreads are incomparably better. Lamb sweetbreads are too small to slice into medallions. Kevin Stannard, my butcher, can now get veal sweetbreads from Smithfield market. This recipe is my attempt to repeat a dish I ate in a restaurant in Paris a few years ago.

- Veal sweetbreads - allow about ¼ lb per person
- 1 packet of dried morels - soak in warm water at least ½ hour before cooking
- 1 onion, finely chopped
- 2 oz unsalted butter
- 10 fl oz of dry white wine
- 5 fl oz of the water in which the morels have soaked
- 10 fl oz of double cream

Put the sweetbreads in a bowl of tepid water for a few minutes to remove any blood. Drain and put in a saucepan of cold water and bring slowly to a boil and boil for about three minutes. Drain once more and put into cold water and remove any little pieces of skin. Drain yet again. Cover with foil, put a plate over them with weights and refrigerate overnight ; they will now be firm enough to cut into slices; they are now ready for cooking.

Soften the onion in unsalted butter. Add the sliced sweetbreads, salt and pepper and fry on high heat, turning the slices over, until coloured. Add the morels and cook for a few minutes more. Now gradually add the white wine and then the morel water and and simmer for 15 minutes; whenever the sauce has reduced too much, top it up with some more liquid. Add the double cream, season and reduce again. The sauce should be unctuous.

Keep warm until ready to serve.

I have cooked this again recently and there was enough left over to reheat for my supper the next day. The flavour seemed to me to have been greatly enhanced, so it seems a good idea to cook this dish the day before and reheat it before the guests arrive

Veal Sweetbreads and Morels

# Basmati rice

There are two basic ways of cooking rice - the Indian and the Chinese styles. In the Indian, boil the rice in plenty of water for 20 minutes, drain, rinse under running hot water; allow to dry; replace in the pan and fluff the rice with a fork. In the Chinese style - (taught to my grandmother, with me watching, by two Chinese gentlemen in Hampstead Garden Suburb in the 1930s) - put some fat (Butter or oil) into a pan, measure the rice (1 cupful for four persons), coat the rice with the fat; add double the quantity of water and simmer slowly until all the water has been absorbed; then fluff with a fork and serve.

# Spinach

I often buy spinach in the vacuum packed plastic bags. I put the bags unopened, one at a time, in the microwave and cook at max temp for 4 minutes. The spinach is then wilted and a nice dark green. If you object to buying vacuum packed spinach from a supermarket, take a good quantity of organic spinach leaves (they are always sold ready washed), put them in a pyrex dish, cover and cook in the microwave at maximum for about 6 minutes (Spinach beet, which is what the organic spinach always is, seems to need longer). Drain the spinach in a colander and cut it roughly with two knives.

Put cubes of pancetta in a pan and when the fat begins to run add a good piece of butter and brown a handful of pine nuts, add a handful of sultanas and now the roughly cut wilted spinach and stir until fully cooked.

I first ate spinach cooked in this way in the restaurant on the roof of the Hotel Tivoli in Lisbon. It was described as being in the Basque manner.

# Rack of lamb

- half a rack of lamb (for 3 people) - about 9 cutlets
- Small potatoes for roasting
- young broad beans

I reckon it will take about 35/40 minutes to roast the lamb at a high heat. I don't think it needs any accompaniment in the roasting dish; just place the lamb on a rack. Roast the potatoes in goose fat in a different dish. If you double the quantity of meat you will have enough to eat cold with salads. Many don't like eating cold fat, but if well cooked it is very good.

# Moroccan lamb tagine

for 5 people

- 2 ½ lbs shoulder of lamb, cut into quite large dice
- 5 tbsps of extra virgin olive oil
- 2 large onions, finely diced
- 2 cloves of garlic, peeled and chopped
- 1 cinnamon stick
- 1 tsp ground cumin
- 1 tsp saffron stamens, or two packets of saffron powder
- 1 tsp powdered ginger
- 1 large bunch of coriander leaves
- 1 small handful of juniper berries
- ½ tbsp of harissa
- 16 slices of preserved lemons (citrons confits)
- ½ lb of pitted green olives
- 1 small bunch of flat-leafed parsley
- 1 tbsp of orange flower water

Marinate the cubed lamb in the bottom of a tagine or a deep titanium braising pan for a good three hours with the oil, onion, garlic, cinnamon, cumin, saffron, ginger, chopped coriander leaves, juniper berries, the harissa and a little salt and pepper (it can be kept in the fridge for at least 24 hours).

It is very important that the sauce of a tagine should be unctuous, so never let the sauce become too liquid. The original recipe said "add enough water to come nearly to the top of the meat"; I now add less than that and keep an eye on it and top up when necessary. Cover the pan and simmer until the lamb is tender - at least an hour (I usually do this the day before).

Reheat and add the lemons, after ten minutes add the pitted olives and simmer for another ten minutes.

At this point, if the sauce is not 'unctuous', I transfer all the solid ingredients with a slotted spoon to the tagine and keep warm and then reduce the sauce and then pour it over the meat.

Keep warm until the guests are ready to eat. My plate warmer actually keeps it just cooking, so check the consistency of the sauce before serving.

At the last minute add the finely chopped parsley and sprinkle with the orange flower water.

Serve with couscous or rice. A green salad goes well with it.

NB Couscous has always given me trouble in the past. Every packet seems to have different instructions and some of them are time consuming and complicated. I have recently discovered a simple solution:

For 5 people. Put two cupfuls of couscous into a deep oven proof dish. Add one and a quarter cupfuls of hot water, stir with a fork and allow to plump for a few minutes. Add the same amount of water again and fork it. Now add four tablespoons of olive oil and fork again. Just before serving 'crumble' the couscous with your hands - just as one would do for the crumble of apple crumble. Now cover the dish and put into a microwave and cook on maximum for 2 minutes 40 seconds. Remove, fork again with a few lumps of butter. Place on plate warmer. As a variation, try adding a few drops of truffle oil or a tablespoonful of truffle flavoured olive oil.

NB Preserved lemons. I have often used bought preserved lemons; there is a brand called Belazu, but they are small whole lemons preserved in water with ascorbic acid. A much better flavour can be achieved with home preserved lemons. Most recipes for preserving lemons call for lemons whole or cut into wedges. I prefer the following recipe.

# To preserve lemons

Thinly slice six unwaxed lemons, discarding the end pieces and any obvious pips.  Lay them on large china platters (nothing metallic) in a single layer. Six lemons take up three of my large platters. Sprinkle them with fine sea salt and leave in a cool place for at least twenty four hours - forty eight hours is OK. Drain off the surplus water. When the lemon slices are limp they are ready to be stored. Dry the slices with absorbent kitchen paper towels.

Layer the lemons in preserving jars, sprinkling each layer with a little paprika. Leave room at the top; pour over mild olive oil and cover the slices with at least $\frac{1}{2}$ an inch of oil. Seal and leave the lemons for at least four weeks before using. They will keep for six to nine months in a cool, dark place. As they age, the lemons mellow and become a beautiful golden colour from the paprika. The oil left in the preserving jars is useful for marinades.

# Cold meats with salads and other accompaniments

# Cold roast duck with salads

I buy Gressingham duck breast fillets (in pairs). The Gressingham is a cross between a mallard and a Pekin duck. I buy them from Friday Street Farm Shop. Coat the fat side liberally with a garlic and ginger purée and cook them for 30/35 minutes in a circo-therm oven (Neff). The fillets go into a cold oven and are then subjected to a stream of hot air (190 degrees Celsius). They are then brown and crisp on top. Remove and allow to cool. Carve in diagonal slices; should be nice and pink. If you don't have a circo-therm oven, roast them on a rack in a hot oven for 20/25 minutes.

# Garlic and ginger paste

Peel all the cloves of garlic from one large bulb of garlic. Peel an equal or slightly larger quantity of fresh ginger root. Chop the ginger and the garlic and place in the bowl of a food processor (the ginger is too tough to risk in a blender). Add one tablespoonful of white wine vinegar. Start to process and reduce to a coarse paste. Now gradually add grapeseed or sunflower oil until you have a paste with the consistency of double cream. Bottle the paste and keep in the fridge.

# Tomato and red onion salad

This is the typical Moroccan salad served with fish on the quayside at Essaouira. Good flavoured tomatoes, sliced, with red onion peeled and very thinly sliced, served with extra virgin olive oil - no vinegar.

# Celeriac remoulade

Half a celeriac is sufficient for four people. Peel the celeriac, cut into chunks and then  slice them into coarse strands in the food processor. Blanch them in  vigorously boiling water for one minute. Strain in a sieve and hold it under cold running water for half a minute. Mix some mayonnaise with dijon mustard and fold into the celeriac, making sure that all strands are liberally coated. Season to taste.

# A Moroccan Tagine

A Moroccan lamb tagine with preserved lemons

# Chicory and beetroot salad

for four people

- 2 heads of chicory (what the French call endive)
- 2 small cooked beetroots
- small handful of walnut pieces, roughly chopped
- 1 tsp of fenugreek powder
- a large dollop of mayonnaise
- *Optional* - two Cox's Orange apples, peeled, cored and sliced - keep fresh with a sprinkling of lemon juice

Cut each head of chicory lengthwise into four pieces and then slice and place in a bowl, peel the beetroots and cut into good size cubes and add to the bowl; add the chopped walnuts and sprinkle the fenugreek over; toss the mixture in mayonnaise.

This is how I have prepared this salad for some time, but just the other day I came across a very old recipe in a book of cuttings from newspapers (dating back at least forty years) and found the same recipe to which was added the apples. Having now tried it, I think it may be better with the apple. Don't allow any vinegar to get anywhere near the beetroot! I should add that my own distinctive contribution to this recipe is the ground fenugreek; that does not appear in any of the old recipes.

# New potato salad

Salad potatoes, (pink fir apple or the like), boiled - should still be firm; slice and mix with home made mayonnaise (Hellman's will do, if you feel lazy); sprinkle with chopped chives.

# Green tomato salad

This is not, as you might imagine, a salad of unripe green tomatoes. A near neighbour grows lots of unusual tomatoes and this one is green when ripe. I use it with finely sliced red onion; it is always a good talking point - 'green but ripe'.

# Rocket, spinach and watercress salad

This is just a tossed green salad using baby spinach leaves with rocket and watercress.

# Chickpea, cauliflower and preserved lemon salad

(This recipe comes from Casa Moro, the second book)
- 1 small cauliflower cut into small florets
- Chickpeas.
- a good handful of fresh coriander leaves
- sea salt and black pepper
- ½ preserved lemon

Casa Moro obviously expect one to cook the chickpeas oneself. For an octogenarian it is too time consuming and really not all that better than a can of chickpeas. Certainly the home cooked are softer than the tinned ones. Although it is not strictly Levantine I often substitute tinned cannelloni beans, which are softer.

½ preserved lemon, inner pulp removed, finely chopped - makes about 1 heaped tablespoon. Here I use my home preserved lemon slices (already described earlier - Moroccan Lamb Tagine) and don't bother to remove the pulp, and finely chop 3 or 4 slices.

### Dressing
- 1 tbsp lemon juice
- 3 tbsps extra virgin olive oil
- 1 tbsp of zaatar (optional). (Being unable to get zaatar locally I use instead a teaspoon of harissa, which goes very well)
- 1 ½ tsps of cumin seeds, roughly ground with a pestle and mortar

Whisk all these ingredients together in a bowl

Casa Moro say "blanch the cauliflower for a couple of minutes or until tender". No cauliflower will be tender enough for me after only two minutes. I boil the cauliflower for precisely six minutes, drain in a sieve and hold it under running cold water for about a minute. Now put the drained cauliflower, chickpeas, preserved lemon and coriander in a large bowl. Pour on the dressing, season with salt and pepper and mix well.

# Tomato salad with mozzarella

Cut the tomatoes in half and then slice them. Put them in a dish, cover them with sliced mozzarella di bufala cheese and plenty of torn basil leaves. Dress with vanilla flavoured olive oil.

# Fennel à la Greque

*(This recipe comes from Jane Grigson's Vegetable Book. I have made two small changes.)*

- 2 medium onions, chopped
- 1 large clove of garlic, crushed
- ¼ pint of olive oil
- 2 tins of Italian chopped tomatoes
- bouquet garni
- 1 teaspoon coriander seeds, lightly crushed with mortar and pestle
- a good splash of dry white wine
- juice of two lemons
- 3 heads of fennel, sliced
- chopped fennel leaves

First make the sauce. Sweat the onions and garlic in oil until they are soft. Then add the tomatoes, bouquet, coriander, wine, lemon juice and seasoning. Simmer for thirty minutes.

In the meantime steam the sliced fennel for ten minutes. Now add the fennel to the sauce and cook for a further five minutes. Remove the fennel with a slotted spoon to a large deep platter. Taste the sauce and reduce if it is copious and watery. Otherwise, correct the seasoning and pour it hot over the still warm fennel.

Cool it and place the platter on a cool marble surface in the larder. Serve the next day and sprinkle with chopped fennel leaves.

Jane Grigson uses fresh tomatoes, whereas I use tins, and adds the fennel slices - blanched - to the sauce after 15 minutes and continues stewing for another 30 minutes. I have tried this and found the fennel still a little too crunchy for my taste.

# Baked potatoes to serve with cold meats

I cut corners with baked potatoes; rub them with a bit of butter, spike them with a skewer and place them on a baking tray just below the grill in a combination oven. Turn on the grill and the microwave at the same time; for one person cook for five minutes, turn the potato and cook again for about four minutes. You have a cooked potato with a crisp skin! For three or more potatoes you need to double the cooking time. But you won't want the grill on for more than ten minutes; so revert to plain microwave after ten minutes. Before serving test for softness by pricking with a carving fork.

# Baked sweet potatoes with feta, olives and coriander

- a small piece of Feta cheese, roughly broken up
- 1 tsp of fennel seeds
- ½ tsp of harissa (the original recipe called for chillies, but I find them too hot)
- 1 garlic clove crushed
- ½ tsp of coriander seeds, crushed with a pestle and mortar
- extra virgin olive oil
- 1 medium sweet potato
- half a dozen pitted black olives
- a small handful of coriander leaves, roughly chopped

Mix the first five ingredients with just enough oil to moisten them.

Bake the sweet potato ( I would never bother with this dish if I had to bake the sweet potato for 50 minutes), I cook it in the microwave for 4 minutes, turn it over and do another 4. Unlike the regular baked potato this does not need a combination oven since there is no need to crisp the skin with the grill at the same time.

Cut the baked potato in half, make incisions in the flesh with a knife and cover with the feta mixture. Top it with the black olives and the chopped coriander.

# Sweet and sour red cabbage to accompany cold meats

Cut a small cabbage into four, cut away the hard core and finely shred the leaves. Melt 2 oz of butter in a heavy pan and add 2 oz of sugar. Stir just to blend and add 4 tablespoons of red wine vinegar. Add the shredded cabbage and toss well to mix the ingredients.

Cover and cook over gentle heat. The slower the cabbage cooks the better it will taste and it can easily be left to cook for two hours. Stir or shake the pan occasionally.

When ready the cabbage should be slightly moist. Add a good tablespoon of red currant jelly and toss to glaze the cabbage.

# Mashed potatoes and sweet potatoes to accompany cold meats

Potatoes cannot be mashed in a food processor; they become glutinous; but a mixture with sweet potatoes can be so mashed. Mark you, it is not much trouble to mash the cooked potatoes with a masher and then to beat them with a fork with milk and butter.

# Stewed marrow to accompany cold meat

Take a young marrow and skin it with a potato peeler. Cut it into round slices. With fingers and thumb push out the seeds and the pith from the centre. Brown a chopped onion in olive oil in a big pan. Now add the rounds of marrow, and stir around. Slice three large tomatoes and add to the pan with a bay leaf. Cover and stew on a moderate heat for half an hour. Check and stir after a quarter of an hour. Serve with a slotted spoon; you won't want all the liquid.

# Sole Florentine

for five people

- 2 medium to large dover soles; get the fishmonger to skin both sides
- 1 large onion
- 1 bay leaf
- 3 oz of grated parmesan cheese
- 2 oz unsalted butter
- plain flour
- ½ pint of milk
- fish stock - see below
- 2 packets of spinach

Fishmongers, and even the fishermen on the beach at Aldeburgh, seem to be very reluctant to fillet the soles for one. So I do it myself. With a sharp knife cut four quarter fillets from each fish. cut each fillet into about four pieces and set them aside.

In a large saucepan soften the onion in melted butter; add the fish heads and the chopped fish bones, the bay leaf and add water to cover. Simmer for twenty minutes - no longer. Drain and set the stock aside. Freshly caught Dover sole is always better after being kept for a couple of days, so I prepare this stock the day before.

Wilt the spinach in any suitable way. Cut the spinach with two knives and place it on the base of an oven proof pyrex dish. Place the pieces of fillet of sole on top of the spinach.

Make a sauce mornay, making a roux with the butter and flour, adding the milk and then 2 oz of grated parmesan cheese. Pour the sauce over the spinach and sole fillets and sprinkle with the remaining cheese.

I then cook this in a very unorthodox way. I place the dish at the top of a combination oven, turn on the grill and at the same time microwave on maximum for 5 minutes. It is now cooked and nicely browned on top. I have recently found that it is an even crisper brown if you sprinkle a little polenta evenly over the cheese.

A more orthodox way would be to fry the sole fillets in butter before putting them on top of the spinach and place the whole dish in a preheated hot oven 190 Celsius for abut 15 minutes, until the top is nicely browned

Serve with new potatoes.

# Dressed crab and lobster salad with Pernod dressing

**Served with green tomato salad, rocket, spinach and watercress salad and new potatoes (hot)**

## Dressed crab

I'm lazy and buy crab already dressed - round here it is always Cromer crab. I always serve it with home made mayonnaise made in the old fashioned way in a bowl with a wooden spoon.

## Lobster salad

Take two medium lobsters, cooked on the beach, cut each lobster in half and remove all the flesh from the body and carefully do the claws, dice the lobster flesh and fold it into the following dressing:

- 5 tbsps olive oil
- 1 tbsp Dijon mustard
- a handful of parsley, tarragon and chives, chopped
- 1 tbsp of finely chopped shallot
- 12 drops of soya sauce
- freshly ground white pepper
- a small glass of Pernod

I discovered this dressing in Jane Grigson's Fish Cookery and she in turn got it from Alexandre Dumas in his Grand Dictionnaire de Cuisine.

# Ragout of Beef

# Ragout of beef

- 1 ¾ lb (750 g)  Chuck steak
- 3 oz piece of fatty bacon 75g
- 12 oz Onions 350g
- 2 tbsp oil
- 2 Tomatoes
- 1 tbsp tomato paste
- ½ tsp. salt
- 2 tbsp flour
- ¼ pint red wine
- ¼ pint hot beef stock
- 1 bay leaf
- 5 white peppercorns
- 8 oz button mushrooms
- 1 green capsicum
- 1 red capsicum
- 2 tbsp chopped parsley
- 2 tbsp brandy or a miniature brandy

Wash and dry the beef. Trim and cube. Cube bacon. Peel and chop onions.

Cook bacon in deep stewing pan until fat runs. Add beef and cook for 10 minutes over a high heat, turning contents over with a wooden spoon after 5 minutes. Add onions and oil. Cook for a further 3 minutes.

Skin tomatoes and chop finely; or, just as good and a little easier, add a can of Italian chopped tomatoes. Stir into the pan with tomato paste and salt.

Sprinkle flour into the pan, stir in well and cook for 3 minutes. Add red wine, beef stock, bay leaf and peppercorns. Cover and simmer gently for about 50 minutes or until meat is tender.

Wipe mushrooms; halve. Deseed capsicums and cut into strips. Add both and cook for 15 minutes more.

Add parsley and brandy, raise heat and cook for 10 minutes, uncovered. Make sure that the sauce is well reduced . The sauce of all stews should be positively 'unctuous'. Leave to stand for 5 minutes before serving.

Serve with new potatoes and a green salad, or with tagliatelle ( the trouble there is that it not easy to keep tagliatelle warm whilst the guests are having drinks and eating the first course).

# Pasta dishes

## Pasta with tuna and tomato sauce with capers

- Linguine - on my own I use 2 oz, with guests I allow 3 oz per person
- 2 tbsp olive oil
- 1 medium onion
- 2 cloves garlic
- 1 tin of Italian plum tomatoes
- seasoning
- 1 can of tuna
- handful of chopped capers
- handful of chopped parsley

Heat the oil and gently fry the chopped onion and garlic until softened. Add the tomatoes with their juice and salt and pepper to taste. Break up the tomatoes with a wooden spoon and cook over a high heat for about ten minutes. At this point some people purée the sauce in a blender; I prefer it more rustic. Add the drained and flaked tuna and capers and cook for a further ten minutes.

Cook the pasta as directed if you want it 'al dente' - I always cook for at least one minute longer than the directions on the packet; I don't like my pasta too aggressively 'al dente'. No cheese with this recipe.

## Pasta and tuna with pinenuts and sultanas

Since a holiday in Sicily in 2005 I have taken to the Sicilian version of pasta with tuna. A small handful of pinenuts is added to the onion and garlic at the beginning and a handful of sultanas with the tuna - no capers. Most Sicilian recipes call for 'raisins', but I am assured that real Sicilians always use the plumper 'sultanas'. Although not strictly Sicilian, I sometimes add a generous handful of frozen garden peas - it adds a touch of colour.

## Pasta with mushroom and fungi porcini cream sauce

Cook pasta in the normal way. In a large frying pan soften a small chopped onion. Add the sliced mushrooms and the sliced dried porcini, which have been soaked for 30 minutes in warm water. Cook over a high heat until cooked, tossing the pan frequently. Add a small amount of the liquid from the soaked porcini until there is a much reduced sauce. Now add a small carton of cream; heat through and serve with pasta.

# Pasta with romanesco cauliflower

**A Sicilian dish - a more subtle flavour**

- 600g pasta (traditionally bucatini – a type of thick spaghetti)
- 1 large cauliflower
- a handful of sultanas
- a handful of pine nuts
- 1 onion
- 6 anchovy fillets
- 1 small packet of saffron
- olive oil
- salt and pepper

Cut up the cauliflower and boil in salted water until soft. In the meantime, gently sauté the chopped onion in olive oil until brown and add the anchovies, the sultanas and the pine nuts. Mix well and leave to cook gently for about 10 minutes until the cauliflower is ready. When cooked, add the cauliflower to the anchovies, onions etc., using a spoon with holes in so that the cauliflower water remains in the pan. Add some of the cauliflower water and slightly mash the cauliflower, mixing it with the other ingredients.

Now add the saffron, salt and pepper and leave to cook gently, making sure it doesn't get too dry. If it does, add more cauliflower water. Just before the pasta is cooked, add the saffron and mix in thoroughly.

Cook the pasta and drain when ready. Serve the cauliflower sauce on top of the pasta and sprinkle liberally with parmesan cheese, or another stronger cheese, such as ricotta salata.

# Linguine with monkfish sauce

A new recipe improvised the other day for supper for four

- 2 oz of linguine per person
- 2 tbsps of olive oil
- a small piece of fillet of monkfish, cut into rounds
- a packet of cubetti di pancetta
- a small handful of pine nuts
- a small handful of sultanas
- a packet of spinach, wilted in any way you choose
- about 5 oz of double cream

This takes no time to do, so start cooking the linguine and then prepare the sauce.

To make the sauce. Wilt the spinach in advance. Spinach in packets is always just leaves, but organic spinach from the Farmers' Market always has stalks. Don't worry about them, just chop them and cook them with the leaves; they soften very quickly.

In a deep stewpan start cooking the pancetta in the oil. Add the pine nuts and sultanas and stir fry for a minute or two; now add the monkfish and stir fry until well cooked. Now chop the spinach and add to the pan, stirring all the while. By this time the linguine should be done and all that remains is to add the cream to the pan, drain the pasta, add it to the pan and heat it through.

# Spaghetti with spinach, cream, parmesan and pine nuts

- spaghetti 3 oz per person
- 2 pkts of spinach, chopped
- ½ pint double cream
- 2 ½ oz of grated parmesan
- handful of pinenuts - lightly toasted
- olive oil

Cook the spaghetti. Heat the olive oil in a deep pan. Add the leaves of spinach gradually, stir frying until the spinach has completely wilted. Now add the pinenuts and the cream, stirring until piping hot. Now add the parmesan cheese and stir until melted. Tip the drained spaghetti into the pan with spinach and stir until coated.

This is a very simple quick supper dish, which (with smaller quantities) I often have when alone.

# King scallops with parsnips and fried leeks with bacon

- 3 scallops per person
- 2 parsnips
- 1 lb of leeks
- 4 oz of streaky bacon
- 2 oz of butter

Peel and cut the parsnips into pieces. Boil until tender and then purée them with butter and milk (as with mashed potatoes). Set aside and keep warm.

Trim away the root and the green part of the leeks down to about 1 inch from the white stem. Split open and wash well, then shred coarsely. Trim and chop the bacon rashers. Melt the butter in a pan and add the bacon. Season well with freshly ground black pepper. Stir and then cover with a lid and cook over gentle heat for about 20 minutes to soften. Keep warm.

Now, in a very hot pan (just moistened with butter) sear the scallops on both sides until nicely browned.

Serve the scallops on a bed of parsnip purée surrounded by the leeks.

# Roast sirloin of beef with roast potatoes and cauliflower Mornay

On this occasion I used a piece of sirloin off the bone. but not rolled - a piece from which one would cut sirloin steaks.

I always time the roasting by using a meat thermometer; it seems to need to roast for a little longer than the temperature indicated for medium rare beef. In 2004 I had not yet discovered goose fat for roasting, but it is much the best fat for roasting potatoes. I like to use small potatoes, leaving the skin on.

Cook the cauliflower as indicated in Granny's Cauliflower salad. Serve with a béchamel to which cheese (parmesan or cheddar) has been added.

# Swordfish steaks Messina Style

for two people

- 2 swordfish steaks (about ½ lb each)
- a good splash of white wine
- a can of peeled plum tomatoes
- ¼ lb pitted green olives
- a handful of desalted capers
- 3 small potatoes thinly sliced
- seasoning
- water
- flour
- parsley

Coat the steaks in flour and sear in a non-stick pan with a little oil until golden brown.

Now for a tricky bit - add a few splashes of white wine; it will spit madly; have some absorbent kitchen paper handy - might be very difficult on a gas hob; I have a ceramic hob which is easily wiped clean. Immediately add the pitted olives, the capers and the peeled tomatoes. Dilute the sauce with a little water or bottled passata. Season with salt and pepper; arrange the potato slices over the fish. Cover and cook over a moderate heat for about 15 minutes.

Arrange the steaks on a dish and cover with the sauce and potatoes. Sprinkle with chopped parsley and serve with blanched samphire (just the tender tips)  Samphire - (Salicornia Europaea) - grows in all the estuary marshes in Suffolk, but I buy mine from Wendy's stall in Saxmundham.

# Roast skate wings

for two people

- 2 half wings of medium size skate
- 1 small onion or shallot
- desalted capers
- plain flour
- olive oil

I copied this recipe after eating the dish at The Captain's Cabin in Aldeburgh High Street.

Finely chop the onion and scatter over the bottom of an oven dish big enough to take the skate wings flat and moisten with olive oil and a small splash of white wine.

Dust the skate wings with plain flour. Scatter a small handful of capers over the fish. Roast in a hot oven for about 25 minutes, basting the fish with the juices from time to time. For the last ten minutes sprinkle a small handful of polenta over the fish. Serve with wilted spinach tossed in butter or oil, to taste.

# Monkfish Tagine

One of my guests did not eat meat, but would eat fish, so I adapted the recipe already given for lamb tagine to monkfish. The only difference is that it needs to cook for much less time; you don't want the monkfish to disintegrate. Including the time for the preserved lemons and the pitted green olives the total cooking time should not exceed forty minutes. Serve with couscous.

# Cratfield sirloin steaks

**Served with chicory stewed in olive oil and lemon juice; new potatoes**

2 local sirloin steaks from Cratfield (Friday Street Farm Shop).

I cook them by the circo-therm method. Brush both sides lightly with olive oil; season well with sea salt and black pepper. Place on a rack in a cold oven and cook for 25 minutes at maximum heat.

2 heads of chicory- cut each head in two, lengthwise.

Heat a deep stewing pan, add 2 tablespoons of olive oil. Place the four pieces of chicory, rounded side down, and fry until turning brown. Turn the pieces over and squeeze the juice of one lemon over them. Cover and cook over a low heat for 15 minutes. Check that they aren't burning and, if necessary, squeeze a little more lemon juice over them. The slight browning of both sides of the chicory gives a delicious flavour.

# Alternative vegetables to have with steak
## Broad beans

Old broad beans are impossible unless you go to the trouble of peeling off the outer skin after they have been boiled. I find this a bore and buy very young broad beans and always include a few of the young pods, which are delicious; don't overcook them and toss them lightly in a little butter. In Catalonia you can buy delicious bottled tiny broad beans; I haven't been able to find them in England or, for that matter, in France. Frozen broad beans from the farm shop are quite acceptable.

## Courgettes

Cut each courgette into about three pieces, cross ways. Place each piece in a contraption for cutting potatoes into chip size. Place all the courgettes 'chips' into boiling water and blanch for about three minutes. Drain and set aside. Just before serving toss the 'chips' in hot olive oil for about three minutes.

# Braised chard

Wash the chard, drain and cut into pieces. Heat some olive oil (vanilla flavoured oil goes very well with chard) in a stew pan, stir fry the chard quickly until wilted, cover the pan and cook slowly for 15 minutes.

# Fillets of lamb stewed with gooseberries

**Served with Linguine or tagliatelle, spinach with pine nuts and raisins**

- 1 fillet of lamb per person
- ½ lb of gooseberries
- a large knob of butter
- 2 large cloves of garlic
- 2 tsps ground cumin
- 1 tsp ground nutmeg
- a very large handful of chopped mint
- 1 tbsp of plain flour
- ¾ pint of unsweetened apple juice
- large bunch of parsley
- a small handful of pine nuts
- a few pinches of cayenne pepper to taste or a teaspoon of harissa

Cut the lamb fillets into 1 inch rounds. Roughly chop the mint leaves. Peel the garlic and chop roughly. Top and tail the gooseberries (I use frozen gooseberries from the Farm Shop and thus avoid the, to me, tedious process of topping and tailing.)

Melt the butter in a deep stewing pan, add the spices and the meat and stir around just to coat the meat and seal. Remove from the heat and stir in the flour with a wooden spoon. Put back on the hob. Gradually stir in the apple juice and bring to the boil, stirring until the juices have thickened. Now add the gooseberries, the chopped mint and the cayenne or the harissa and some salt to taste.

At this point the original recipe says cover and put the casserole in the oven at 170 C for 1 ½ hours. As readers will know, I prefer to continue with my deep stewing pan on the hob, simmering for about an hour and a half. Stirring from time to time and checking that the juices have not gone too dry.

Chop the parsley finely and toast the pine nuts in a little butter to brown them. Just before serving stir the parsley into the stew and scatter the toasted pine nuts over the surface.

I have to admit that on several occasions I have at the last minute forgotten the pine nuts. It is still very good, but misses a rather special touch.

Linguine and spinach recipes already given. On a very recent occasion I served with this 'fruitful stew' couscous and sautéed cardoons - just a bit more special.

# Cardoons

Cardoons are best picked after an overnight frost, but they can be cut at anytime. Cut the stalks at ground level, with a sharp knife, strip off the grey leaves, leaving only the white stalks, cut these into chunks like chard; place them immediately in a pan of cold water with the juice of one lemon to stop them discolouring.

Drain, cover with fresh water and sprinkle two tablespoons of flour into the water. Bring to the boil and then simmer gently for about 20 minutes until tender. Drain and cut the cardoons into cubes. Sauté them quickly in butter until golden.

Alternatively, put the chunks into a food processor with butter and cream and process until you have a smooth purée.

# Baked Sea Bass

- 1 locally caught sea bass, about 1 ½ lbs (for three people)
- 1 sprig of fennel leaf
- 1 bay leaf
- a splash of white wine
- 2 tbsps of olive oil
- spinach
- new potatoes

Heat the oven to 190 Celsius. Ensure that the fish has been descaled and place it on a piece of foil large enough to wrap the whole fish in. Put the herbs inside the fish. Sprinkle it with white wine, moisten it with the olive oil. Wrap the foil round the fish sealing it and place in the oven to bake for 25 minutes. Unwrap and serve with the vegetables.

# Pheasant or guinea fowl in a cream sauce

In a deep bottomed stewing pan brown the bird(s) in hot butter or goose fat. Add one finely sliced onion. Turn down the heat and cover - no need to add any liquid, leave to braise for 45 minutes.

Add a small carton of double cream, the juice of half a lemon and (optional) half a pound of small button mushrooms, halved - double this if you are cooking two birds. Continue cooking, covered, at a low heat for another 15 minutes.

Carve the fowl, cutting off the legs and then carving the breast. Place the carved bird on a platter and pour over the cream sauce. (Katie Stewart's original recipe does not call for mushrooms and calls for the sauce to be strained, but I like the bits of caramelised onion.)

# Roast beef for lunch on Christmas Day

- Roast rib of beef on the bone
- Roast potatoes in goose fat
- Stir fried Brussels sprouts in cream

### Roast beef
The important thing here is the beef. I picked out the piece of beef at the butcher's (Kevin Stannard of Saxmundham) as early as mid-November. It had already been hanging at least two weeks. So by Christmas Day it had been hanging for at least seven weeks. It was quite superb and melted in one's mouth. Roasted the normal way, resting on a bed of chopped onions and sliced carrots and spiked with a meat thermometer. When it reaches the right temperature let it rest and make a gravy with the pan juices adding a good splash of red wine.

### Stir fried Brussels sprouts
This recipe came from a newspaper and called for the prepared sprouts to be finely shredded (using the blade of a food processor). I prefer it less finely shredded (the coarser blade). Heat some olive oil in a deep pan and stir fry the sprouts for 1 to 2 minutes if finely shredded, rather longer if more coarsely. Add a generous splash of white wine and continue to stir and cook over a high heat until it evaporates. Pour in a ¼ pint of double cream, add seasoning to taste (Salt, pepper and grated nutmeg) and let the mixture bubble until the sauce reduces slightly - 2 to 4 minutes.

# Romesco de peix

**A Catalan fisherman's stew**

- 6 tbsps olive oil or, even better, avocado oil
- 1 large Spanish onion, roughly chopped
- 2 garlic cloves, thinly sliced
- 2 dsps finely chopped fresh rosemary
- 3 bay leaves
- 2 red peppers, quartered, seeded and thinly sliced
- ½ tsp sweet smoked paprika
- 1 400g tin plum tomatoes, roughly chopped
- ¼ pint white wine
- saffron strands, infused in 4 tbsp of boiling water
- 5 ½ oz whole blanched almonds, lightly toasted and roughly ground
- 1 ½ lbs of monkfish fillets cut into chunks about 2 in square
- 1 lb of clams

There are many more complicated recipes for this dish, particularly for making the Romesco sauce. But the sauce is the key and I have found this recipe very successful, but the secret is not to rush it. Before the fish goes in the sauce must have acquired a rich creamy texture with a most delicate flavour.

In a large stewpan heat the oil over a medium heat. Add the onion and a pinch of sea salt and cook, stirring now and again, until golden and sweet - about 15-20 minutes. On no account proceed to the next stage until the onion is really golden (as in onion marmalade).

Add the garlic, rosemary, bay leaves and red pepper. When the pepper has become really soft - at least ten minutes - add the paprika and the tomatoes and simmer for another ten minutes. Now add the white wine and cook for another two minutes before adding the saffron infused water. Finally thicken the sauce with the toasted almonds roughly ground in a pestle and mortar.

When you are almost ready to eat add the monkfish and clams. Cover and simmer until the fish is cooked through and the clams have steamed open (about five minutes). Serve with new potatoes and a fennel salad.

# Roast chicken with lemon and rosemary

A recipe taken from the Daily Telegraph. It's a most unusual recipe; the herbs are scattered over the finished chicken, instead of roasting with them. Such simple treatment calls for truly tasty chicken. The recipe called for 2 smallish free-range hens (about 1 ½ lbs each). I could not find birds small enough and bought two larger corn fed chickens.

Cut the chickens in half down the length, removing the backbones with poultry scissors. I don't have poultry scissors and it was the devil of a job to remove the backbones with a very large kitchen knife. I have since changed the recipe and buy ¼ chickens from the Sutton Hoo chicken farm in the farmers' market.

Preheat the oven to 250 C. Line a large roasting tray with baking parchment and layout the chicken quarters skin side up. Rub each one with softened butter and season liberally with salt and pepper - nothing else.

Bake the quarters for 25 minutes without turning (no more and no less), this produces wonderfully crispy skin. Allow to rest for 10 minutes before serving

Meanwhile destalk 2 sprigs of rosemary and a small bunch of parsley. Peel the zest from one lemon and chop everything together as finely as possible. Just before serving scatter the chopped herbs and lemon over the chicken pieces.

No gravy required, just squeeze some lemon juice over the chicken. Serve with:

# Potato and garlic chives cakes

- The recipe called for wild garlic, which I don't seem to find around here, so I use garlic chives which I have growing in the garden.
- 2 large floury potatoes
- 2 tbsps butter
- 2 tbsps whole grain mustard
- salt and pepper
- 1 egg, beaten
- 4 tbsps polenta
- 5 tbsps vegetable oil

Boil the potatoes in plenty of salted water until they are very tender. Drain and mash the potatoes with the butter and the mustard. Allow the mash to cool thoroughly and season. Chop the chives and stir them into the potatoes with the beaten egg.

Spread the polenta on a chopping board. Dollop dessertspoon sized pieces of of the potato mix on top of it and sprinkle with more polenta. Working very gently, roll or pat the potato into patties or rissole shapes, so that the outsides are thoroughly coated with polenta.

Heat the oil in a large frying pan and brown the potato cakes on both sides until crisp, ensuring that they are piping hot in the centre.

# Roast Monkfish with port and chervil sauce

*(This is a recipe I got from going on a cookery course at Hintlesham Hall in 1992 run by the head Chef, Alan Ford.)*

for six people

- 6 pieces of trimmed fillet of monkfish
- 3 rashers of streaky bacon
- 3 large onions - peeled and cut into fine strips
- 2 oz butter

## For the sauce
- 2 shallots - roughly chopped
- 1 pint of fish stock (monkfish bones do not make fish stock - so have some stock made previously from a cod's head and bones)
- 6 tbsp of port
- ½ oz of butter
- ¼ pint of double cream
- some chopped fresh thyme
- a bay leaf
- a good handful of chopped chervil

Cook the monkfish first. Cut the bacon into thin strips (lardons); make incisions in the monkfish and insert the bacon. Seal the monkfish on all sides in butter and place in an ovenproof dish. Cook in a hot oven for about five minutes; set aside and keep warm.

Now cook the onions. What you are going to make is onion marmalade. Cook the onions in a hot pan on top of the stove, stirring regularly, until it is caramelised and golden brown.

## To make the sauce
Sweat the shallots, without colouring, with the thyme and bay leaf. Add 5 tbsp of port, reduce, add fish stock, reduce, add the cream and reduce until it has the correct consistency (a good creamy sauce), now add the remaining port season and strain. Finally add the chopped chervil

To serve, put the monkfish on top of the onion marmalade and surround with sauce. Delicious!

# Fricassée of turkey with smoked eel and soured apples

*(This recipe comes from Michael Smith's New English Cookery.)*

- 1 ½ lbs boned raw breast of turkey cut into 2 inch strips
- 8 oz smoked eel fillets, cut in the same way
- 4 fl oz Amontillado sherry
- 4 fl oz single cream
- 2 oz unsalted butter
- 2 green apples
- Juice of half a lemon
- seasoning
- noodles or tagliatelle to accompany

Peel, core and trim the apples, and cut in 6 wedges. Toss in the lemon juice, and drop them, with the lemon juice, into boiling salted water and simmer for 1 ½ minutes. Drain and put on one side.

Heat half the butter and fry the turkey pieces in it in 2 or 3 batches until lightly browned on both sides. Transfer each batch to a warm dish (adding butter as needed).

Deglaze the pan with the sherry, letting it bubble for a minute or two. Pour in the cream and let it bubble until beginning to thicken. Carefully mix in the strips of turkey and smoked eel and heat through until well coated with the sauce.

Serve garnished with the apples on a bed of noodles or tagliatelle.

Don't forget the apples. I once served this dish and returning to the kitchen later found the apples, still set aside! The dish was still admired, but would have been even better with the apples!

# Fillet of Lamb Buxlow

(First cooked for three in October 1992 - quantities can of course be increased proportionately for more guests)

- 3 shoulder fillets of lamb cut into rounds
- 3 shallots
- 2 tsps ground cumin
- 1 tsp cinnamon
- 1 tsp turmeric. (Many consider turmeric the poor man's saffron, but I find it has an attractive distinctive flavour and colours the dish a good yellow. Moreover I have very recently read that turmeric has an ingredient that dramatically reduces the likelihood of developing Alzheimer's!)
- 1 tsp salt
- 6 slices of preserved lemons
- ¼ pint dry white wine
- ¼ pint chicken or vegetable stock

Chop and sweat the shallots in oil, add the lamb rounds and brown over a high heat. Now add the spices and stir for a minute. Add the slices of preserved lemon and pour in the wine and reduce. Add the stock and bring back to the boil.

At this point in 1992 I transferred the casserole to a medium oven for 45 minutes. Now with my titanium stew pan I simmer the stew on the hob for 55 minutes until the meat is tender and the sauce reduced to an unctuous consistency. If you use the oven you need to transfer the casserole back on to the hob to reduce the sauce to the right consistency.

Serve with tagliatelle and steamed courgettes, cut into 'chips', tossed in olive oil.

# Stuffed marrow

for three people

- 1 medium marrow - it needs to be young; it is all right if you can easily press your thumbnail into it.
- 1 ½ lbs of minced beef or minced lamb to taste
- 1 onion finely chopped
- 3 rashers of streaky bacon, chopped
- 1 tin of chopped tomatoes
- 3 squirts of tomato purée
- 1 cup of beef stock (a cube is fine)
- *optional* - 1 large black spored mushroom
- 4 oz of butter
- enough flour to make a roux
- ½ pint of milk
- 2 ½ oz of a strongly flavoured cheese (Emmenthaler, Comté or parmesan)

Most recipes for stuffed marrow call for a complicated process of tying the marrow together with string. My method avoids that.

Cut the marrow in half lengthwise. With a large spoon scoop out all the seeds and the pith. Pre-cook the marrow as follows. Place the two halves skin side up on a rack over an oven pan with a half pint of water in it. Cover the marrow halves with a sheet of foil. Place in a preheated oven - 180 Celsius - for half an hour. Check with a two pronged fork that the marrow is tender, but don't allow it to over cook, so that it disintegrates. Remove from the oven and set aside.

In the meantime cook the chopped bacon and the onion in olive oil until turning brown, for added flavour add the sliced mushroom, now add the mince and stir fry until the rawness has gone. Now add the tomatoes, the tomato purée and the stock and cook for half an hour. Virtually all the water should have evaporated.

Fill the marrow halves with the meat mixture, letting it rise above the level of the halves.

Now make a thick cheese sauce and pour it over the marrow halves. The meat and the marrow should be completely covered. Put the marrow back into the oven for half an hour and serve.

# Frankfurters and apple

Line the bottom of a small oven proof dish with frankfurters (3 per person). Spread them generously with prepared English mustard.

Peel and core one or two cooking apples (Bramleys). Slice them thinly. Soften them in butter and demerara sugar (or honey) in a frying pan.

Place the apples over the frankfurters. Sprinkle the mixture with grated cheese. Put one or two tablespoons of chicken stock (Knorr liquid is very convenient) in the dish and bake for half an hour in the oven at 180 C.

## Stuffed Marrow

# Egg dishes
## Omelettes

55 years ago I was taught to cook an omelette in the French style by a former colleague in the Bank of England, whose mother was French. An omelette he said had to be 'baveuse' (literally 'dribbling'); the omelette must not be allowed to set fully as in a Spanish omelette.

The essential piece of equipment is an omelette pan, which on no account is to be used for any other purpose. The one I have used for some years now is the one mentioned by Delia Smith which led to a surge in sales for the company which saved it from going bust. I think it may have been a Lakeland Limited pan.

To make an omelette (for one person and adjust suitably for more).

I favour cheese or ham or mushroom omelettes. Whichever it is, prepare the filling first. For cheese, simply coarsely grate an ounce or two of cheese. For ham, just chop a couple of slices of good ham. For mushrooms, slice two or three mushrooms, sauté them in a separate pan. Beat the eggs lightly with a fork; don't season them; seasoning is best done at the table when it has been cooked. Heat the dry pan over a high heat. Now add a knob of butter; it should sizzle loudly and immediately turn brown; tip the pan to cover the whole surface. Now pour in the beaten eggs and add the filling over the top. With a spatula keep withdrawing the cooking egg from the sides, tipping the liquid into the space vacated. Whilst still 'baveuse' turn one side of the omelette over the other and tip, out on to a plate.

Serve with buttered toast.

## Scrambled eggs with mushrooms

The recipe for scrambled eggs has already been given, when served with gravadlax. Before scrambling the eggs, prepare the mushrooms. Sauté the sliced mushrooms in a pan with a chopped garlic clove; when the mushrooms are colouring, add a splash of white wine and reduce until there is less than a spoonful of sauce.

Serve alongside the eggs with buttered toast.

# Ballindalloch chicken

Returning from France I broke my journey at a B & B near Canterbury. The hostess was a very good cook and provided a delicious dinner. The main course, chicken, was exceptionally tasty. My hostess said she had got it from "I Love Food" by Clare Mackintosh-Grant Russell, the laird of Ballindalloch Castle on Speyside. She lent me the book for bedside reading. The recipe came under this title. I have memorised the recipe as best I could and have tried it twice since my return. Here it is (for one; increase the quantities for more):

*   1 boned chicken breast (I use Sutton Hoo chicken with the skin on)
*   a large knob of butter
*   1 slice of good ham
*   1 onion coarsely chopped
*   3 squirts of tomato puree
*   ½ a tin of chopped tomatoes (not in the original recipe, but I have found it improves the sauce)
*   5 fl oz of double cream
*   1 oz of grated parmesan cheese

Pre heat the oven to 170 Celsius (fan assisted) - otherwise 180 C. Fry the chicken breast in the butter until brown on both sides. Place it in a shallow oven proof dish. Cover the breast with the slice of ham.

Now fry the onion in the same pan until just browning. Remove the onion and put it on top of the chicken breast and ham.

Still in the same pan add the double cream, three squirts of tomato puree and half the tin of chopped tomatoes; stir it round to amalgamate and pour over the chicken. Put the grated cheese over the top and bake in the oven for 20 minutes.

Serve with new potatoes and a suitable vegetable, green beans, braised chard or spinach.

# A rather special supper for one

(Special because it can only be cooked in the month of May, when St. George's mushrooms are in season.)

- a sirloin steak
- organic chard
- a baking potato
- dried St. George's mushrooms
- grated cheese
- butter

This was a spur of the moment menu. I was in the butcher's in Saxmundham and said 'have you got a piece of really well hung sirloin?". The butcher emerged from the cool room with a piece of sirloin on the bone with the outer flesh almost black. "Wonderful", I said, "cut me a nice steak".

I already had a packet of Peakhill farm chard in the larder and a few days earlier I had found some rather old St. George's mushrooms, already rather dry. I had put them on a windowsill for a couple of weeks and they were now completely dry.

To cook, soak the dry mushrooms in a little warm water; cook the steak - 21 minutes at maximum heat in the circotherm oven (or otherwise grill it in your usual way); chop the chard and stir fry in vanilla flavoured olive oil and then cover and turn the heat down and allow to braise.

Bake the potato - 9 minutes in a combination oven, with the grill and microwave at the same time, turning it over after 4 ½ minutes. Cut it in half, and cut the flesh with a sharp knife. Dot it with knobs of butter and sprinkle it with grated cheese.

Drain the mushrooms and fry them in hot butter; when brown, add some of the water in which they have soaked and cook until the water has completely evaporated, cover the baked potato with the mushrooms.

It was a quite delicious supper. I am sure it would also be nice with some other wild mushrooms, but probably not ceps - too strong a flavour.

There are two morals to this recipe. Don't be afraid to improvise and do talk to your butcher; a butcher always responds well to a customer who wants to know where the meat comes from and how long it has been hung.

# Puddings
## Tropical fruit pavlova

- the whites of four eggs
- 8 oz of caster sugar
- 2 teaspoons of corn flour
- 1 teaspoon of white wine vinegar
- A generous half pint of whipping cream - at least 300 mlls
- 2 passion fruit
- 1 ripe mango
- 1 ripe papaya

Preheat the oven to 200 degrees celsius. Whisk the egg whites until stiff in a food processor - better too stiff than not stiff enough; while still whisking add the caster sugar a tablespoonful at a time add the corn flour and the vinegar and whisk briefly again. Place a sheet of baking parchment on a baking tray, rubbing it with butter so that the meringue mixture will not stick. Put the meringue mixture on the baking tray with a spatula, smoothing it into a level circle.

Place in the oven and immediately reduce the heat of the oven to 115 degrees celsius. Leave to bake for an hour and a half. Turn off the oven and leave the meringue in for another hour or two.

Turn the meringue upside down on to a large enough plate and peel off the baking parchment. This can be prepared several days in advance and stored in the larder.

To serve, whip the cream until stiff, spread over the meringue with a spatula. Halve the passion fruit and spoon the seeds and juice over the pavlova; peel and slice the mango, cut the papaya in half, scoop out the seeds with a teaspoon, peel the fruit and slice onto the pavlova.

Pavlova is perhaps even better with passion fruit alone. The slight acidity of the passion fruit is particularly well suited to the sweetness of the meringue. Another good pavlova, in season, is with raspberries.

I got this recipe whilst channel hopping on digital TV and found Nigella Lawson describing how to make a pavlova. Most household cooks must know the secret of using corn flour and vinegar; yet I have eaten many pavlovas with an unpleasant chewy interior to the meringue. If you follow the recipe above I guarantee that the meringue will always be crisp. The secret must be to put the meringue mixture initially into a very hot oven - 200 C, as above.

# Eton Mess

- 1 lb of strawberries
- meringues
- 10 fl oz of double cream, whipped quite firm

Follow the meringue recipe for Tropical Fruit Pavlova, but halve the quantities of egg whites, sugar, corn flour and white vinegar; and put the mixture on to the baking parchment in tablespoonful dollops (not all one piece).

To serve, cut the strawberries into halves and leave them in a large serving bowl. Crumble the meringue pieces into large chunks and sprinkle over the top. Just before serving add the whipped cream and fold the mixture together.

# Brandy croissant pudding

- 3 one day old croissants
- 1 tbsp chopped, mixed peel
- ¾ pint of creamy milk (I use a little less milk and top it up with single cream)
- 2 eggs
- 2 oz of caster sugar
- ½ tsp of extract of vanilla
- 2 tbsps of bandy (or one miniature bottle)
- Butter and sugar to finish

Butter an ovenproof dish. Slice the croissants in half, lengthwise, and arrange them in the dish, sprinkling the mixed peel over them evenly.

Beat the milk. brandy, eggs, vanilla and sugar together and pour over the croissants. Allow to stand for 1 to 2 hours ( or even longer). Just before cooking, dot the pudding with butter and sprinkle with a little more sugar. Bake in a preheated oven 180C for 50 to 60 minutes until well risen and golden brown. This is as good as any bread and butter pudding that I know of.

This is still very good when cold. If I do it for myself it will do one hot supper and two cold ones.

# Oriental fruit salad

Nothing could be simpler. Peel, deseed and slice a papaya. Peel a mango and slice the flesh off the stone. Peel and slice a small sweet and ripe banana. Mix all the fruit together and place in the fridge just before lunch - no need for any dressing.

# John Gott's baked pears

- 2 oz of melted butter
- 4 peeled halved pears
- ¼ pint of double cream
- 3 tbsps Poire Williams

A very simple pudding. Pour half the butter and half the sugar into an ovenproof dish. Lay on the pears. Add the remaining butter and sugar and bake in a preheated oven (220 C) for 20 minutes. Pour over the cream mixed with the liqueur and bake for a further 20 minutes.

# Spiller's raspberry pudding

- 1 ½ lbs fresh or frozen raspberries
- ¼ lb Digestive biscuits
- 2 oz unsalted butter
- ¼ lb demerara sugar
- 1 pint thick cream

Crush the biscuits and mix with melted butter. Allow to cool. Stir in the sugar. Whip the cream very stiffly. Arrange the ingredients in a glass bowl in layers as follows:
- Cream
- Raspberries
- Biscuit mix
- Cream
- Raspberries
- Biscuit mix

# Chocolate pots

**'Petits pots de chocolat à la crême'**

- 6 oz. of good quality cooking chocolate (Chocolat Menier)
- a generous ½ pint of single cream
- 1 egg
- 1 pinch of salt
- ½ teaspoon vanilla essence

Break the chocolate into small pieces and place in the goblet of a blender. Heat the cream until just on boiling - do not let it boil. Add the cream to the blender and blend until smooth - the heated cream melts the chocolate. Break the egg into the goblet, add a pinch of salt and the vanilla essence and blend again. Pour into ramekins (6); it will still be quite liquid. Chill in the fridge for at least 8 hrs. Serve with crème fraiche.

# Pumpkin Pie

*Adapted from Mrs. Rombauer's Joy of Cooking for use with food processor.*

- 3 tablespoons soft brown sugar
- 1 tablespoon caster sugar
- 1 teaspoon cinnamon powder
- $1/2$ teaspoon ground ginger
- $1/4$ teaspoon ground cloves
- $1/2$ cup maple syrup (Mrs Rombauer says 'corn syrup', but I can't get it here)
- 3 eggs
- 1 $1/2$ cups cooked or canned pumpkin
- 1 $1/2$ cups double cream
- 1 teaspoon vanilla essence or 2 tablespoons brandy or rum

Line a 9 inch fluted baking dish with short crust pastry. Preheat the oven to 200 degrees celsius.

Mix all the ingredients thoroughly in the bowl of a food processor. Pour the mixture into the baking dish.

Bake in oven for about 50 mins - check that it is done by sticking a 'silver' knife in - if it comes out clean, it is done. I usually at this point turn the oven off and leave it in the oven for another ten minutes.

It will keep in a cool larder for several days.

To cook a pumpkin, I cut it in half, scraping out all the seeds, and cook one half at a time. Pour some water into an oven pan and place the half pumpkin, skin side up, on a rack over the water. Bake at around 180 degrees (fan assisted) until tender. Remove from the oven and cool. Scrape the pumpkin flesh from the skin.

I then measure 12 ounces of flesh (equivalent to 1 $1/2$ cups). I then freeze all the pumpkin not used immediately in 12 ounce packs for future use - either in pumpkin pie or in pumpkin risotto.

# Brandy butter for Christmas pudding

- 6 oz of unsalted butter
- 8 oz of sieved icing sugar
- 1 miniature bottle of brandy

Cream the butter until soft, then gradually beat in the icing sugar. Beat in the brandy very thoroughly. Pile roughly into a serving dish and chill well before serving.

As an added touch you can add a little finely grated orange zest.

The table set for dinner

# Index